TRAMS, BUSES & TROLLEYBUSES
Past and Present

No 2 SUSSEX

TRAMS, BUSES & TROLLEYBUSES

Past and Present

No 2 SUSSEX

Michael H. C. Baker

Past & Present Publishing Ltd

First published in 2012

British Library Cataloguing in Publication Data

A catalogue record for this book is available from the British Library.

ISBN 978 1 85895 276 5

Past & Present Publishing Ltd
The Trundle
Ringstead Road
Great Addington
Kettering
Northants NN14 4BW

Tel/Fax: 01536 330588
email: sales@nostalgiacollection.com
Website: www.nostalgiacollection.com

Printed and bound in the Czech Republic

All photographs are by the author unless otherwise credited.

For Kate Melvin who now knows far more about the bus routes of Sussex than she could ever have imagined.

CONTENTS

Nothing for your author could be more evocative of Southdown as he remembers it in the immediate post-war years than the subdued but powerful roar of a Harrington-bodied TS7 or TS8 Leyland Tiger setting off from its stop at Thornton Heath Pond as it headed down the A23 on its way from Victoria Coach Station to Brighton. On 14 November 2010 No 1179 perfectly recreates those sounds and sights as it turns out of Pool Valley on to the Promenade; after passing the Palace Pier it will swing through 190 degrees, then head north along the Steine.

A little later that never-to-be-forgotten sound fills the air again as TD5 Titan No 248 follows No 1179 past the Palace Pier.

INTRODUCTION

Think of Sussex Buses and almost automatically that means Southdown: think of locations and that means Brighton. Well, you will find plenty of pictures of both within these pages, but there is much more besides. Certainly Southdown dominated the scene in its glory days before being swallowed up by the National Bus Company. Its territory stretched westwards across the Hampshire border, north to link with Aldershot & District and London Transport at such pleasant market towns as Midhurst, Horsham, Crawley (pleasant? – well you decide) and East Grinstead, eastwards into Kent at Tunbridge Wells, and almost within sight of France at Hastings.

As for Brighton, it has a good claim to be Britain's first and finest seaside resort – although the citizens of Scarborough might disagree – holiday home of the Prince Regent and Queen Victoria until the arrival of the great unwashed – in her eyes – by train drove her across the water to the Isle of Wight, motor buses having not been invented in the 1840s. A city since the year

2000, Brighton is a place long celebrated for its sense of style, whether in architecture, dress, outrageousness or whatever, where just about anything goes.

I have lived in Sussex twice, in West Sussex in Bognor, and later in East Sussex in Hailsham. I was brought up in Thornton Heath in the London suburbs, and beautiful leaf-green coaches, usually Harrington-bodied Leyland Tigers, their ownership displayed in bold gold manuscript, passed the bottom of our road each day on their way to and from the Sussex coast. It was possible to book a seat on one at the local newsagent round at Thornton Heath Pond, and on several never-to-be-forgotten occasions we did just that, arriving at the poky little coach station at Manchester Street some 2 hours later, having paused at the rather grand County Gates refreshment rooms at Crawley – built in 1931 for the not inconsiderable sum of £10,000 – on the A23.

My primary school bus-spotting friend, Clive Gillam – now, some 60-odd years later, a resident of New South Wales – recalls a journey from Thornton Heath to Eastbourne and back:

'On a typical summer Saturday, 58 Southdown services passed Thornton Heath Pond. They ran principally to Brighton, Eastbourne, Seaford, Worthing and Littlehampton. Southdown coaches also operated on the shorter Beacon Motor Services run to and from Crowborough. It was at the end of my summer holiday in Eastbourne in 1949, aged 11, and I was being seen safely on to a Southdown Express Service. It was at the bustling Cavendish Place Coach Station and there was barely an inch of parking space that wasn't covered by a coach or passengers milling around. Inspectors and drivers alike were patiently attending to their passengers' needs.

I had been staying as usual with my Grandfather Gillam. I had wanted to make the return journey from Eastbourne to Thornton Heath, where I lived, by stage carriage service. My grandfather would have none of it. I suppose it was my own fault. I had indeed travelled that summer from Thornton Heath to Eastbourne by bus.

The journey had entailed boarding a red London Transport 133 to West Croydon and a green 409 to East Grinstead. From there the Southdown service 92 operated directly to Eastbourne. It was not until the 92 entered Eastbourne that I realised I was an hour later that I had stated in my letter to my grandfather. He met me with a mixture of relief and annoyance. I had made a simple error in reading the timetables for the planned change from 409 to 92 at East Grinstead.

Now, after my seaside holiday, it was time to return home, not by bus but by coach. My disappointment only deepened when I was sent up the steps of the 1930s-built RELIEF coach to occupy the last remaining seat, the aisle seat of a three-seater opposite the rear door. From it I had a good view of the entire aisle to the front bulkhead. Oh misery me! The journey of some 2½ hours thankfully ended when we arrived at Thornton Heath Pond.

The door slid back revealing my good friend John Willard with his Dad's homemade wheelbarrow. My small case was retrieved from the locker by the driver and I thankfully put it in the wooden barrow. My fellow passengers witnessed this small ceremony with much hilarity! On the longish walk home to Norbury Avenue I spent the time recounting the time spent "spotting" at Eastbourne.'

Knowing that I was putting this book together, Clive consulted his Southdown timetable Down Under and recorded the activity at Cavendish Place in the high summer of 1951. Coach movements numbered 41. Half of these were South Coast Express services jointly operated with the East Kent Road Car Company. The 41 services exclude the ubiquitous RELIEF coaches provided to meet the usual holiday demand for extra seats. This would have been the very last summer when the half-cab coach was ubiquitous. Southdown's very first underfloor coaches, Duple Ambassador-bodied Leyland Royal Tigers, were delivered in May, but these were luxury touring coaches and would not have been used on express services. Many more Royal Tigers for express services, with Leyland, Duple and Harrington bodies, would arrive in 1952.

Harrington, which had its factory at Hove, and Southdown not unnaturally worked closely together, and a succession of beautiful-looking examples of the coachbuilder's art was the result, from the mid-1930s until the firm closed in the 1960s. Southdown specialised in coach tours, both home and abroad, and many of the coaches it used were luxurious in the extreme, with two-by-one seating and retaining quiet, smooth-running petrol engines, after diesels had become otherwise standard. But times move on, and the Plaxton Panorama coaches mounted on Leyland Leopard chassis in which I used to travel between Hailsham and London in the late 1960s were worthy successors, and a good deal more relaxing and comfortable than the Morris Minor, which was my conveyance at other times. One appreciates the loss felt when Southdown colours were superseded in the 1970s by the all-embracing National white, yet this did create a brand image that appealed to the travelling public, and it has to be said that the modern coach has a turn of speed that would not only have left its predecessors standing but also most family cars, while its great height affords excellent views of the Sussex countryside.

From 1929 until 1967 the standard Southdown double-deck bus chassis was the Leyland Titan in its many variations, although the Guy Arabs that the Government foisted upon the company

Above right: **This is the Southdown Coach Station in Cavendish Place, Eastbourne, in 1976. There is precious little genuine art deco architecture in the United Kingdom, so it is nothing short of extraordinary that** Southdown should have possessed two art deco coach/bus stations, at Bognor and Eastbourne, the only ones in the country so far as I know. The tragedy is that both should have been wantonly destroyed. In one's blacker moments one sometimes assumes that any distinguished architecture built in an English seaside town since the Second World War – and I *don't* mean the sort of which Prince Charles would approve – only got past the planning department of the local authority while it was sleeping off a liquid lunch.

Left: A preserved Southdown Leyland PD3/Northern Counties open-topper, No 410 of 1964, on its way to the top of Beachy Head, heads up Cavendish Place towards the sight of the former coach station and garage on 7 August 2011.

during the Second World War were, on reflection, found to be not half bad, and further examples were acquired between 1948 and 1956. Bodywork came from a variety of manufacturers, particularly in the immediate post-war period when most of the TD3, 4 and 5 Titans were given replacement bodies, but the apple green and primrose livery with dark green lining ensured that they all exuded that distinctive Southdown air of quality. The full-fronted PD3s, nicknamed 'Queen Marys', have gained a following among enthusiasts, both because of their longevity and the fact that a number have been preserved, although personally I never thought them particularly handsome. I considered the Park Royal-bodied Atlanteans of 1974/75 superior; they would have looked splendid in traditional Southdown livery. The NBC era of the ECW-bodied Bristol VR, a decent enough, reliable, old-fashioned vehicle, and the best forgotten Leyland National single-decker, was one that not surprisingly saw a decline in bus travel and sent the enthusiast community into deep depression.

Stagecoach, which took over Southdown in 1990, has gradually pulled back from many parts of Sussex and abandoned practically all the former Southdown premises. Companies such as Metrobus, Countryliner and Renown have stepped into the breach, but, interestingly, Stagecoach's greatest presence is in Worthing where, more than 100 years ago, Worthing Motor Services started up, becoming Southdown in 1915.

Although Southdown was far and away the biggest cheese in Sussex, three other BET concerns, Aldershot & District, Maidstone & District and East Kent, worked into the county, as did London Transport. Trams operated beside the seaside in Brighton and Hastings, their systems and the little four-wheel cars that operated them being replaced by trolleybuses – almost silent and streamlined (well perhaps not the early Hastings ones)

– in the 1930s. Eastbourne was the world's first municipality to operate motor buses – applause please. Brighton, ah, Brighton deserves a new chapter.

Not only did Brighton Corporation operate trams, then trolleybuses and motor buses, but the town was also served by Thomas Tilling's Brighton, Hove & District. I had not at first realised that the two were separate, for their red and cream liveries were identical, although I should have known better for, by the mid-1950s, the latter was a keen operator of ECW-bodied Bristols, while the Corporation favoured AECs. Eventually the Tilling concern was swallowed up by Southdown in NBC days, and the Corporation misguidedly adopted a pale blue livery, which, like the NBC green, did not wear very well. Privatisation saw the emergence of the Brighton, Hove Bus & Coach Company, which would by the middle of the first decade of the 21st century become the jewel in the crown that Southdown had once assumed. Its routes spread far beyond the City of Brighton and Hove, some of them once operated by Southdown, notably to Lewes, Tunbridge Wells and Eastbourne. A livery of basically red and pale cream recalled days gone by, but was designed by Ray Stenning's Best Impressions and thus totally of the 21st century. Buses were named after notable Brighton inhabitants, ranging from world-famous statesmen and stars of stage, screen and radio to good men and women who have improved in various ways the lives of their fellow citizens – all part of an imaginative publicity drive that has seen the graph of the growth of bus travel in the city climb steadily and reap a number of well-deserved awards.

We also feature at some length the buses at the Amberley Museum. The uniqueness of this institution is a reflection of the uniqueness of Southdown. With the sole exception of London Transport, no bus company in all of the United Kingdom, perhaps anywhere, is better represented in preservation than Southdown, and it is the skill and dedication of those remarkable men and women at Amberley that has led the way for some 40 years in ensuring that vehicles from the very earliest days of the Southdown company, which came into existence in 1915, have not only been saved from the scrapyard, or in many cases

farmyard, but are once again restored to working order. Indeed, there is at least one bus that predates the formation of Southdown, having been put into service by its predecessor, Worthing Motor Services of 1909, whose green livery Southdown adopted.

Midhurst

We begin at Midhurst, a seriously picturesque town, also famous as the one-time home of H. G. Wells, who was apprenticed to a chemist here and later taught at the grammar school before becoming just about the most successful author of his time. On 11 January 1979 a couple of Southdown PD3s take a rest in the car park at Midhurst between performing school duties.

Today the buses have moved a few yards south and are seen here at the bus station on 11 January 2011. The toilets and tourist office can be glimpsed on the extreme right, and also on the right of the earlier picture. On the extreme left is a Countryliner Dennis Dart, then a Mercedes

minibus of the Midhurst Community Bus, then two Stagecoach vehicles, No 3524, a Dennis Dart working route 1 to Worthing, and Scania Enviro 400 No 15586 on route 60 to Bognor Regis.

Aldershot & District 32-seat Strachan-bodied Dennis Lancet J3 No 909 of 1947 stands in North Street, Midhurst's principal thoroughfare, ready to set off, appropriately, for Aldershot, on 6 February 1956. Despite being served by a network of bus services and possessing a railway station, long since gone, it is quite possible back in those immediate post-Second World War days that the elderly gent inching his way towards the camera might have seldom left his home town.

The Dennis Lancet continued to be bought by Aldershot & District until 1950. One example from that year, Strachan-bodied, 38-seat Lancet J10 No 178 (HOU 904), has been preserved, as seen in the second view.

Finally, in North Street in January 2011 the handsome, less-than-a-year-old Scania Enviro 400 No 15586 is seen again, on its way to the terminus of route 60 at the end of the street; the route indicator has already been altered for its return journey to Bognor Regis. Running every 30 minutes, the section of the journey between Midhurst and Chichester through the heart of the South Downs is worth every penny of the free ticket (actually paid for by many decades of tax contributions) we pensioners were granted by that nice Mr Blair!
P. Trevaskis/MHCB (2)

13

Petworth

Were it not for the East Lancs-bodied 1954-vintage Dennis Lance of Aldershot & District standing here in the Square at Petworth, one might, with a certain stretch of imagination and possessed of a fully paid-up artistic licence, convince oneself one was in a Tuscan hilltop town. Set high above the surrounding countryside and composed of a maze of narrow streets populated mostly by antique shops, the most prominent building in the town is the magnificent Petworth Place, where William Turner had a studio. Turner visited Italy and was much influenced by the light he found there, managing to infuse many of his Sussex paintings with that same glorious, shimmering luminosity, which in turn was to be taken up by the French Impressionists. The date is 30 March 1958, the last day that double-deckers operated route 51 to Critchmere, a village just beyond Haslemere.

The Dennis Lance was something of a rare beast beyond Aldershot & District territory. The oldest surviving working example – indeed, the oldest working Aldershot & District vehicle – is this one, No 145, a Lance 3 dating from 1950 and fitted with an East Lancs lowbridge 51-seat body. *P. Trevaskis/MHCB*

On 12 May 1966, Southdown East Lancs-bodied Titan PD2/12 MUF 457 of 1953 and Aldershot & District Northern Counties-bodied AEC Reliance 393 AOU of 1961 meet in the Square. The uncharacteristically untidy blind of the Titan makes it difficult to make out that this is actually a short working of the long route 63 from Chichester, 51 minutes away, to Horsham, 1 hour 3 minutes further on.

In Petworth Square on 11 January 2011 very little seems to have changed over the years apart from the erection of a small bus shelter and the consequent moving of the back door of the Town Hall. The bus is a Stagecoach Southdown Transbus Pointer 2 of 2006, working the hourly route 1 from Worthing to Midhurst. *P. Trevaskis/MHCB*

Horsham

This page: At Horsham Garage on 5 May 1955 is this open-top Brush-bodied Leyland TD1 Titan of 1929, serving as a tree-lopper. When this veteran finished its passenger service in 1950 virtually no modifications were needed, other than the removal of most of the seats and repainting in an all-over grey livery. It was scrapped later in 1955. Most fortunately, an identical vehicle, UF 4813, has been preserved, initially by Southdown, and lives at Amberley Museum – we shall meet it a little later.

Horsham Garage closed in January 1987, and this is the site in Denne Road, with the railway line passing behind it, in January 2011.

Opposite page: Horsham Garage was used in the wintertime to store coaches and open-top double-deckers, and basking in the sun in May 1955 is No 1410 (BUF 990). Many Southdown aficionados consider the 1400s, Leyland TS7 and TS8 Tigers with Harrington dual-purpose bodies, built between 1935 and 1939, the highpoint of half-cab single-deck bus design – anywhere. No bias there, for although they were essentially buses they were perfectly capable of performing coach duties, and regularly did. No 1410 entered service on 31 October 1935, had its petrol engine replaced by a diesel one in 1942, and was sold out of service in August 1956. Many became standee buses during the war (although not this particular one), with 30 seats around the perimeter, allowing another 30 standing

passengers; your author's only journey in such a vehicle was to Horsham in 1941. Next to it is No 496, a wartime utility Guy Arab with a Park Royal body, although it was actually delivered in March 1946, seven months after the war ended. In 1952 it was rebuilt as an open-topper to replace the ancient Short Bros TD1s (see opposite). No 496 will shortly be relicensed and take up work conveying holidaymakers from Eastbourne to the top of Beachy Head, and will continue to work until 1964; usually wartime buses had a pretty short life on account of their poor bodies. Although it is sad that none of the magnificent 1400s have been preserved, an open-top Guy, No 451, was brought back to Sussex from Denmark in 2001 and is being restored. On the right is a pre-war Morris 8 van.

The 2011 view is from the site of Horsham Garage, looking across Denne Road.

At Carfax, the heart of Horsham, on Saturday 13 October 1956, London Transport RT 767 is working the 434 service to Roffey on the eastern edge of the town. This bus is painted in Central Area red, for at that time it was common for Country Area routes to be so oversubscribed on fine weekends that vehicles were sent from the Central Area to help out.

One of the most distinctive sights at Carfax in the immediate post-war era was one of these handsome PD1s of Hants & Sussex, working the Roffey route. Hants & Sussex

was owned by the redoubtable Basil Williams, who from the 1930s onwards operated a network of small bus and coach companies in Sussex and Hampshire and was a distinct thorn in the side of Southdown and London Transport. This particular PD1 is working a service to Thorney Aerodrome – many of Basil Williams's most profitable routes were those serving military establishments.

The local route to Roffey is now worked by Metrobus, and that company's No 398, a Dennis Dart SLF with a Plaxton Pointer body, formerly of London & Country and delivered in 1997, is seen taking on passengers.

The fourth picture shows Basil and Mrs Williams at their Emsworth home shortly before Basil's death in 2001. *MHCB/Author's collection/MHCB (2)*

When I first knew Horsham in the 1940s it was very much a market town, serving the surrounding rural community, but although there are still whole streets of handsome ancient buildings dating back to medieval times, by the 21st century it has taken on much more of the feel of outer suburbia. Although Leyland was always the favoured chassis supplier for Southdown, the company was impressed by the wartime Guy Arabs and bought a number more in the 1940s and early 1950s. Brand-new No 513, delivered in March 1955, stands at Carfax, the heart of the town, working trunk route 17 to Brighton. The Park Royal 57-seat body with platform doors and drop-down windows was a perfect match for the Guy radiator, the ensemble being a thing of passing beauty.

On 23 February 1990 Southdown Bristol/ECW VR No 256 (JWV 256W) of 1980 is ready to depart from Carfax for Worthing.

As seen on 18 January 2011 the north side of Carfax has been pedestrianised, and buses stop on the east side. Curiously, while the bandstand remains, the war memorial has been moved.

Horsham was the one place in Sussex, and anywhere else for that matter, where Southdown, Aldershot & District and London Transport all met. On a damp December day in 1968 London Country RT 4763 overtakes AEC Reliance No 549 of Aldershot & District. The Horsham to Guildford route of the latter company benefited from the closure of the railway line between those two towns in the summer of 1965.

One of these rather attractive Metro-Cammell-bodied Reliances, No 543, identical to that in the previous picture, has been preserved and is seen here in Winchester, the western extremity of the company's territory.
P. Trevaskis/MHCB

In the foreground at Carfax in 1971 is Southdown Park Royal-bodied Tiger Cub No 642 of 1955, and behind is London Country RF 588 of 1953. Note the distinctive bus stops of each company; it has to be admitted that the one inherited from London Transport is the most stylish, a legacy of the 1930s when London Transport under the genius of Frank Pick led the world in transport design.

In the second view an elderly gent puffs away in Carfax in 1972, oblivious to RCL 2260 of Reigate Garage. It is one of the splendid Routemaster double-deck coaches, downgraded from Green Line work but ideal for lengthy journeys through the Sussex and Surrey countryside working London Country's 414 route to West Croydon. It is being passed by Southdown Northern Counties-bodied Leopard No 455.

Thirty-nine years later, on 18 January 2011 another elderly gent stands by the new bus station as a Stagecoach Dart pulls out.

For the 21st century Horsham acquired a

rather fine bus station, designed by Chetwood Associates and erected at the junction of Worthing Road and Black Horse Way, although Carfax is still much used. Metrobus No 390, a Dennis Dart SLF with Plaxton Pointer bodywork, reverses out in January 2011.

Chichester

Chichester was, until Brighton was so elevated in the 21st century, the only city in Sussex. Its origins, as its name would suggest, go back to Roman times; there are the substantial remains of a fine Roman villa at Fishbourne, on its western outskirts on the Southbourne Road, with some of the best-preserved mosaics anywhere in the United Kingdom. Chichester itself has been the ecclesiastical and administrative centre of West Sussex for the best part of 2,000 years, full of handsome buildings, many of them featuring flint and dominated by the cathedral.

On a warm May afternoon in 1955 Southdown Leyland Titan TD5 No 195, dating from 1938, stands opposite the cathedral working a relief on the busy, 4-hour-long 31 route connecting Southsea and just about every place of significance along the coast to Brighton. This is our first meeting with one of the numerous pre-war Titans, which served Southdown so well for some 40 years, from the earliest open-top examples of 1929 to the final 1939-vintage TD5s. Many were rebodied after the war, but No 195 retains its original Beadle body, albeit rebuilt by the same firm in 1946. It was withdrawn in 1956, but some rebodied examples lasted into the early 1960s.

Stagecoach South Trident No 18525 (GX06 DYA), working Coastliner route 700, the successor to route 31, stands opposite Chichester Cathedral in the summer of 2010.

Leyland National 405 DCD was delivered in 1981, and later received the registration formerly borne by a PD3. It is seen here at the same location, looking west, in the apple green and primrose livery, an approximation of traditional Southdown colours, that began to be applied in 1986 but which all too soon gave way to Stagecoach stripes in late 1989.

This 28-seat MCW Metrorider, originally of Cedarbus and seemingly without a registration plate, is in Stagecoach livery but with a Southdown fleet name. Behind it, outside Chichester Cathedral, is a Leyland National in leaf green and cream. Chichester Cross can be seen in the background in the summer of 1990.

At the same location in January 2011 is a successor to the Metrorider, GX58 GJZ, one of the very popular Stagecoach South Optare Solos, with P279 VPN turning in front of the Cross.

There was a time in the 1980s when the Southdown fleet seemed to be composed almost entirely of Bristol VRs and Leyland Nationals, hardly exciting fare at the best of times and made even more depressing by a livery of dull National green, which seemed to start fading the day after it was applied, quite often accompanied by the lettering going the same way, as if ashamed to have replaced the glories of former times. Nevertheless the VRs, even if they did look like something designed in the late 1940s, served the company well and were much improved by the application of Southdown green and cream, as seen here on No 275 of 1981 beside Chichester Cathedral ten years later, working route 260 to Midhurst.

Twenty years later, in January 2011, the route has once again become No 60 and is being worked by one of the very handsome Stagecoach South Enviro 400s, dating from 2009.

Chichester Garage in Southgate, handily placed close to the railway station, was completed in 1956 and was Southdown's largest. Standing outside in 1973 is No 1743, a Harrington Cavalier-bodied Leyland Leopard of 1962 in original green livery, ahead of a Weymann Castilian-bodied Leyland Leopard of 1963, newly painted in National white. Harrington bodies, produced in Hove, will for ever be associated with the heyday of Southdown coaching, and the firm never produced a finer design than the Cavalier. Weymann coaches were much rarer, but the Castilian was distinctive and elegant. Chichester Garage is one of the few inherited from Southdown to have survived into the 21st century.

Ahead of the garage, Southdown built a bus station complete with offices, etc, and that too is still in use by Stagecoach. In 1996 two Alexander-bodied Olympians dating from 1990 are seen at night, with the garage in the background.

The third picture, dating from February 2011, shows a Stagecoach Solo, and an Enviro 200 Dennis Dart of 2010 working Coastliner route 700.

Bognor Regis

In this view from the pier in around 1938, on the promenade are a Southdown Short Bros-bodied Leyland Titan TD1 of 1931 and a Harrington-bodied Leyland TS7 Tiger of 1936 with roll-back canvas roof centre-sections, one of the very last group of coaches to sport this somewhat archaic feature.*Author's Collection*

In the distance in the view from Bognor Pier in October 2010 is a Stagecoach South Dart heading eastwards. Having lived at Bognor as a very small child in 1940/41 I've always had a soft sport for the resort, but honesty compels one to admit that architecturally it is quite the least distinguished town anywhere on the South Coast. Its two greatest claims to fame are that King George V convalesced here, although the rumour that on his death bed, when informed by Queen Mary that if he recovered they would return to the Sussex coast, he replied, 'Bugger Bognor' may or may not be true; and the Tony Hancock film, *The Punch and Judy Man*, was filmed here. *Author's collection/MHCB*

One of the very few buildings of distinction in the town was the beautiful art deco bus station, from which all-Leyland PD2 No 382 of 1948 is emerging on 11 June 1961. Designed for Southdown by Clayton and Black of Brighton, it opened in 1934. Stagecoach closed it in 1982 and, despite a fight by some brave souls, the local authority, whose aesthetic sensibilities over the years would have made Donald Trump blush with shame, let it be demolished.

This is the same location in January 2011, with Stagecoach South Enviro 400 GX10 HBC bound for Brighton.

Bognor Bus Station lives on in miniature in the form of a 1/72 scale model produced by Kingsway Models.

There was a large parking area behind Bognor Bus Station. On 11 June 1961 the unique Leyland Titan PD2 North Counties-bodied double-deck coach No 700 of 1950 is parked ahead of an East Lancs-bodied TD5 Titan. No 700 was a interesting experiment. I used to see it when new passing the end of our road on the London to Eastbourne service, but, perhaps fortunately, I never travelled in it, for it rolled ferociously and also lacked power, so that it was soon demoted and at Bognor was used on school and private-hire work.

Today, as seen in this February 2011 picture, the whole area is a car park.

Leyland Titan TD5 No 215, rebodied by East Lancs in 1950, heads west along Bognor High Street, also on 11 June 1961, about to pass the bus station on local service 55. This was a typical duty for the final pre-war Titans at this time, their last full year in service. Despite its years No 215 still looks pretty good. It had started out with a lowbridge 52-seat Park Royal body in March 1939, but in this picture has a highbridge one. The rebuilding of many bridges some ten years later meant that the need for lowbridge buses was much reduced. The rear of another TD5 can just be seen turning out of High Street

This is Bognor High Street in January 2011. A highly decorated Stagecoach South Enviro 200 Dart leaves no doubt as to which service it is working. In the distance an Enviro 400 is approaching.

Arundel

Sussex is rich in much-loved, picturesque historic towns, but even so few can match Arundel. Set on the southern slope of the South Downs looking across the flood plain of the Arun to the sea, it is dominated by two spectacular buildings, the Roman Catholic cathedral and the castle. The latter is the home of the Duke of Norfolk, the Earl Marshall, England's senior peer of the realm. In the summer of 1998 Stagecoach Volvo/Alexander No 614 of 1994, M614 APN, takes on passengers outside the Norfolk Arms; whether they include the noble duke or any of his family I cannot say.

Just moving off on its way to Brighton in January 2011 is Stagecoach South Enviro 200 Dart GX10 KZK.

Another Volvo/Alexander dating from1996 crosses the River Arun at Arundel in 1997.

Standing in the same position on 8 August 2011, but swinging the camera to look back at the town, Stagecoach South Dart GX10 KZM sets off for Brighton.

Amberley Museum

And so we come to the Amberley Museum & Heritage Centre. Set in a former chalk pit cut into the South Downs, it is a fascinating repository of relics, artefacts and, especially, working examples of our industrial past. But for the bus enthusiast it is first and foremost home of the unique Southdown Omnibus Trust. This was set up in 1998 but its history goes back to 1959, when the first bus in the collection was acquired. There is simply nothing in the country, perhaps nothing in bus preservation anywhere in the world, quite like Amberley, and we tell something of its story in this section of the book.

Here we are crossing the River Arun on the approach to the museum in Southdown No 813. This is the sole survivor of 23 Brush-bodied Leyland Titan TD1s of 1929; we have already seen another example in the tree-lopper at Horsham. The Titan, designed by G. J. Rackham, was the first truly modern double-deck bus chassis. No 813 was preserved by Southdown upon withdrawal from passenger service and passed to Stagecoach, who still looked after this veteran when this picture was taken in 1999, but later placed it on long-term loan to Amberley.

The centrepiece of what makes Amberley so special is the Southdown bus garage. This perfect replica, filled with genuine artefacts rescued from all over Sussex and beyond, is home to a remarkable collection of vehicles. In this picture in front of the garage on the far left is No 813, in the centre is Southdown No 125, and behind it Southdown No 135. It illustrates the quite remarkable antiquity of the buses that either live at Amberley or visit during the annual bus event each September. No 125 might be compared to the broom that has had three handles and four brushes. It originated as a normal-control Leyland N-type single-decker built immediately after the First World War, in 1920, and fitted in 1928 with a double-deck Short Bros body. The body was sold in 1934 and became a summer house; it was discovered in 1972 and brought to Amberley, the chassis having long since been broken up. A similar one, dating from 1923, was found, and the body, containing many of the original parts, mounted upon it; the bus passed its MOT in 1976, took part in the London to Brighton Historic Commercial Vehicle Club run in 2000, and is regularly in service at Amberley. No 135 (CD 7045) possesses an almost identical Short Bros 1928-vintage body mounted on a Leyland N chassis dating from 1922, belongs to Stagecoach South and is presently housed at the Scottish Bus Museum at Lathalmond. The remarkable coming together on that September day in 1997 of Nos 125, 135 and Tilling-Stevens No 52, meant that there were no fewer than three double-deckers of archaic normal-control design giving rides to the public.

The Southdown waiting room and office are seen on a June evening in 1996, with neatly chalked boards advertising excursions. Deane Clark, formerly in charge of restoring historic buildings in Hampshire, is talking to Michael Plunkett, one of the founders and key restorers at the museum.

of both body and chassis are original and it can claim to be the most original surviving pre-First World War bus and the only one still carrying passengers. It has twice completed the London to Brighton run.

Bill Thornycroft, another of the Amberley stalwarts, is in charge of No 52, the oldest surviving Southdown bus. This has a Tilling-Stevens TS3 petrol-electric chassis and a body dating from around 1908. The bus originated with Worthing Motor Services in 1914, the body having been built by its owner, Mr Newman, who ran it in London. Worthing Motor Services became Southdown in 1915, and the bus continued to work until 1927 when the body was sold and became a garden shed in Bognor. Brought to Amberley in 1982, it was mounted on a correct-vintage Tilling-Stevens chassis; much

This little chap, Southdown No 517, is a 30cwt Dennis with a 19-seat Short Bros body dating from 1927. Known as a 'chaser', it was bought at a time when there was little regulation and such vehicles ran ahead of rival operators who were attempting to cream off traffic; the 1930 Traffic Act put an end to this. No 517 was sold in 1932, the body was bought after 50 years as a garden chalet to Amberley, united with an appropriate chassis (a seemingly easy-sounding process that actually involved a vast amount of research and engineering) and put back into service in 1997.

This Tilling-Stevens chassis was once Southdown open charabanc No 67. Dating from 1923, as can be seen in this 2009 picture it has been restored to running order and, as I write, is having a replica body constructed at Amberley.

Perhaps the most extraordinary bus at Amberley is this, Tramocar No 1. Its chassis is original, and its body a replica of one of a fleet of 14 such vehicles that ran along the seafront at Worthing between 1924 and 1938. An early version of a low-floor bus, it is based on a Shelvoke and Drewry chassis, normally used as dustcarts and gully-emptiers, which explains the tiny wheels and tight turning circle. It has very simple controls, rather like those of a tram, hence its name, and would have found it difficult to outpace an averagely nimble horse, which was no handicap for the task on which it was employed. Tramocar was taken over by Southdown in 1938. Tramocar No 1 was launched by the Mayor of Worthing in 1994, the year this picture was taken. Standing beside it is one of the Tramocar drivers of the 1930s.

One of the endearing features of the annual bus day in September is the fleet of elderly pushbikes that provide transport for the staff. Here Bill Thornycroft pursues TD1 Titan No 813.

Tilling-Stevens was one of Britain's leading manufacturers of bus and coach chassis until Rackham's Leyland Titan and Tiger and the AEC Regent and Regal rendered its products obsolete virtually overnight, although the firm struggled on into the 1950s. No 1205 is a 40hp Express model with a Short Bros 31-seat body dating from 1930. At that time the first Tigers were already entering service, but the bus served Southdown successfully throughout the 1930s, being requisitioned, together with all of Southdown's remaining Tilling-Stevens buses and coaches, by the War Office in 1940. After the war it became a home for chickens near High Wycombe, came to Amberley around 1990 and is seen here making it

first appearance after restoration in September 2010.

In a picture that epitomises how authentically a long-gone world can be recreated at Amberley, the conductor collects the fares as 1920-vintage Leyland No 125 negotiates its way down a Sussex lane on a late summer day in 1997.

The period from 1930 to the late 1950s marked the heyday of Southdown coaching, whether on stage carriage services between the Sussex coast and London or on tours through the United Kingdom, Ireland and abroad. A visitor to Amberley in September 1994 was No 4, a Leyland Cub of 1936. It was originally fitted with just 14 seats – armchairs would be a more precise description – and with its quiet petrol engine it was a most refined vehicle.

Southdown referred to all its vehicles as 'cars', but it was a particularly apt description of No 4. Later it was upseated to 20 and fitted with quarterlights to enhance the view of the passing scenery.

Two rebodied Southdown Titans sit companionably side by side at Amberley in September 1997. On the left is No 970, a TD3 of 1934, originally fitted with a Short Bros highbridge body, which was replaced by an East Lancs example in 1946. On the right is No 248 dating from 1939, whose Park Royal body was replaced, again by Park Royal, in 1950. We shall meet No 248 again later.

Although Amberley makes a point of owning nothing later than 1931, more modern Southdown vehicles are always a feature of the September line-up, as seen in this 1997 view of one of the final batch of PD3s. There were 285 altogether, delivered between 1958 and 1967. No 347 is one of the final Panoramics with wide side windows and wrap-around front upper deck windows, a not altogether successful attempt to modernise what was by then becoming a somewhat dated design. No 347 actually got to the breaker's yard, but was rescued and restored over a three-year period by Eric Stobart.

A number of PD3s had removable open tops for summer seaside work; their successors were a batch of ECW-bodied Bristol VRs such as No 603 (TPN103S) seen here. It was one of 30 that entered service with Southdown in National Bus Company days in 1977/78.

Above: **Over the years since the National Bus Company banished apple green and primrose, various anniversaries have been an excuse to revive it. Here Stagecoach Dart No 32501 commemorates Southdown's 90 years at the 2005 bus show.**

Below: **Occasionally rides beyond the confines of the museum have been a feature of the annual bus show, and here in September 1998 two Southdown open-toppers, a VR and a PD3, pass each other on the road between Amberley and Storrington, which runs along the edge of the Downs.**

Littlehampton

East Lancs-bodied Leyland PD2/12 No 789 of 1956 crosses the old Littlehampton swing bridge on its way along the coast from Brighton to Southsea in 1959. These Titans were almost the very last half-cab double-deckers put into service by Southdown – there would be a final eight in 1957. They were a worthy conclusion to a most distinguished line.

The swing bridge was replaced by this retractable pedestrian one in 1973, seen here on 1 February 2011.

Traffic was catered for by a new fixed bridge, some half a mile upstream, seen here on the same day with Stagecoach South Enviro 400 GX10 HBF crossing while working route 600, the successor of the 31.

Worthing

A line-up in Worthing Garage in 1997 features DAF and Ford trucks, a VR under wraps, a PD3 in traditional Southdown green and primrose livery, and a Leyland National in Stagecoach colours. The second view shows the exterior of the garage in February 2011.

The clock that stood for many years above Southdown's Worthing Garage, 1997.

Where it all began. The present garage – or rather garages, for there is more than one building – dates from 1920, but this building, now listed, had been occupied by Worthing Motor Services, which became Southdown in 1915. As can be seen it is today the headquarters of Stagecoach South.

No 440, a Guy Arab with a Northern Counties body delivered in 1944, is seen on the Marine Parade seafront at Worthing in 1950. With Leylands unavailable during the Second World War, Southdown had to take whatever was available and between 1943 and 1946 exactly 100 Guy Arabs entered the fleet. The bodies were built to strict specifications, well below Southdown's peacetime standards. Some even had wooden seats. Various improvements were carried out after the war, and a number, including No 440, were rebuilt as open-toppers and lasted until 1964. In the distance is the Dome Picture House.

By the Dome in February 2011 is Enviro 200 Dart GX10 KZK taking on passengers on its way from Brighton to Arundel. Worthing has a rather impressive seafront, and the row of buildings along Marine Parade are of considerable historic and aesthetic importance; however, much of it was very nearly lost when developers wanted to demolish the Dome and the buildings around it and were given the go-ahead by the council, which had already approved an ugly sports centre to the west. But an enlightened group of citizens fought tooth and nail, eventually a new, more sympathetic council was elected, the developers gave up and went away, and the money was found to restore the buildings.

Worthing played a key role in the very early days of British cinema and it would have been a tragedy if the Dome, dating from 1912, had been lost. It played a central role in the award-winning 1987 David Leland film *Wish You Were Here*, as did, remarkably and surely uniquely, Worthing Bus Garage, which is immediately behind the Dome. Starring Emily Dickenson and Tom Bell, the film was set in the immediate post-war era and restored Southdown buses featured in a number of scenes.

Shoreham

Stagecoach Leyland National HUF 579X travels along the seafront near Shoreham in September 1998.

Preserved Southdown Panoramic PD3 No 347 is seen at the same location in the summer of 1997.

Brighton

Towards the end of the NBC era coaches not in National Express white were allowed some variation, and here Plaxton Panorama-bodied Leyland Leopard No 1358 of 1981 wears what became known as Venetian blind colours as it motors westward along Brighton seafront, Kingsway, towards Hove in 1983. The closure of the Harrington works a mile or so away in Old Shoreham Road, Hove, in 1966 will always be regretted, but the Plaxton Panorama body was a worthy successor to Harrington traditions and a real classic.

The ECW-bodied VRT may not have been the most exciting double-decker ever produced, but Southdown liked it and owned more than 200. The first came out in 1969, early enough to wear traditional Southdown apple green and primrose, and later examples sported variations of this when the NBC released its grip on the company. No 671 of 1979 is seen across the road from the previous picture in 1983.

It was amazing how much more attractive, however briefly, the ECW-bodied Bristol VR looked adorned in apple green and primrose, as No 673 of 1979 again demonstrates in 1986 on the Marine Parade, the A259, above Madeira Drive.

The central works of Southdown was at Victoria Road, Portslade, opened in 1928. Seen inside on 22 May 1956 is Leyland Cub No 15. This Park Royal-bodied 20-seat bus was delivered in the summer of 1936 and put to work on local routes in the Horsham area. It has pretty certainly made its last revenue-earning journey for the company; there is no blind in the rear indicator, and five months later it was sold to a Lancashire dealer. Beyond is a Morris Commercial lorry, and beyond that No 195, a Leyland TD5 Titan, delivered in June 1938. It retains its original Beadle lowbridge body and, like the Cub, is withdrawn and awaiting disposal, which came in September of that year. It ended, as did so many Southdown and Brighton Corporation buses, at J. Lights breakers yard in Lewes.

The second picture shows Portslade works in 1977, in the NBC era. Two coaches are being attended to: nearest the camera is No 1819, a Duple Commander IV-bodied Leyland Leopard of 1970, next to a Plaxton Panorama-bodied Leopard. In the background is a VR.

The works were sold in 1987, and the third view shows the site of Portslade Works in March 2011.

This is Brighton station shortly before the end of the tram system in 1939. Tram No 2 takes centre stage, and in the left background is one of the Thomas Tilling open-staircase AEC Regents, identical to those operating in London. Tilling had arrived in Brighton in 1915 and had established a network of routes. Over the years the Corporation made moves to acquire these routes, but preferred to enter into agreements. Under a 1938 agreement the trams were to be replaced by trolleybuses and a uniform red and cream livery would be adopted for both Corporation and Tilling vehicles. Although the Brighton electric tram system was complete by 1904, trams to the more or less original, four-wheel, open-top design continued to be built, astonishingly, by the Corporation until 1937. One of these, No 53, has survived, and is now being restored and will one

day, it is hoped, be on display at Amberley. Brighton is the most distinguished of all large South Coast railway stations, both inside and out, and has been a natural focus of tram, trolleybus and motor bus routes.

The second picture *(opposite)*, dating from 1983, shows No 469, one of the somewhat clumsy-looking NCME-bodied dual-purpose Leopards delivered to Southdown in 1969, painted in NBC green and white. It is bound for clifftop Peacehaven.

Outside the station about to head down Queens Road towards the sea in 1995 are No 704, a Brighton & Hove Scania Omnicity of 1988, and Brighton Blue Bus Leyland Lynx No 95 of 1990. Brighton Corporation renamed itself Brighton Blue Bus in 1970 and was taken over by Brighton & Hove in 1997. I've always had a soft spot for the Leyland Lynx, for it was not only the last all-Leyland single-decker but also a rather handsome vehicle, and much

better-looking than its National predecessor. Its production career was cut short when the once great Leyland Motors failed and was taken over by Volvo.

Right: Brighton & Hove has in the 21st century been recognised as one of Britain's most go-ahead and successful bus companies. A nice touch is the naming of its vehicles after famous characters associated with Brighton and, Brighton being the unique place it is, there is no shortage of candidates. Open-top Dennis Trident/East Lancs No 819 is seen here in 2009 in Queens Road bearing the name of Max Miller, the 'Cheeky Chappie', one of the most popular comedians of the last years of music hall.

The second photograph shows the man himself – or a more than passable lookalike!

Plaxton Panorama Elite-bodied Leyland Leopard No 1831 of 1971 was part of the last batch of coaches delivered in traditional Southdown livery. Some ten years later a number reacquired this livery and No 1831 is seen on the promenade, Kings Road, Brighton, in 1983.

A virtually new Maidstone & District Volvo B6 with Plaxton bodywork of 1994, wearing the livery that succeeded NBC green, heads along Kings Road. There are some magnificent buildings along the seafront in Hove and Brighton – the monstrosity past which No 3609 is hurrying is not one of them.

No 34, a Brighton Corporation Metro-Cammell Orion-bodied PD3 of 1968, carries an advertisement for Brighton's most famous department store of the time, and has therefore conveniently positioned itself outside said store in 1977.

Hanningtons has ceased trading, but its name survives as can be seen above the Brighton & Hove Scania Omnidekka in April 2011.

Churchill Square is the principal bus boarding point in Brighton, superseding Pool Valley of former years. Brighton was the furthest west that Maidstone & District penetrated into Sussex, on the joint service from Tunbridge Wells and Gravesend. No 5896 (F896 DKK), a Northern Counties-bodied Leyland Olympian of 1988, has just arrived from Tunbridge Wells in 1994 and is about to be overtaken by a Corporation Lynx.

In the second picture a former Green Line coach of London & Country, B290 KPF, a Leyland Tiger with a Plaxton Paramount body of 1985, departs from Churchill Square, Crawley-bound in 1991.

Finally YN54 OBX, a Scania Omnidekka demonstrator, stands in Churchill Square in 2005.

Ever since the arrival of public transport in Brighton it has circumnavigated the Old Steine in the heart of the city, which was once the area where fishermen dried their nets, and today is still an open space of lawns, paths, flower beds and seats set immediately back from the Palace Pier. This is the scene at the west side of the Steine in 1965. No 802, a

Southdown East Lancs-bodied PD2 of 1956, leads No 33, a Brighton, Hove & District ECW-bodied Bristol FSF Lodekka of 1961.

Brighton Corporation bought a fleet of Weymann Orion-bodied Leyland PD2s in 1959, and most of them seem to be on parade beside the Stein in 1961, led by No 52.

Independent Southdown bought 12 Northern Counties-bodied Volvo B10Ms in 1989, specifically for the prestige routes along the coast. They were the very last turned out in traditional apple green and primrose livery, Stagecoach Holdings buying the company in August 1989. No 304 is seen in the third photograph when new at the Steine about to set off on the 4-hour journey to Southsea.

In 1968 Southdown swapped some of the FLF Lodekkas it had inherited from Brighton, Hove & District for eight 33-foot-long Bristol/ECW VRs imported from foreign parts, i.e. Scottish Omnibuses of Edinburgh. The fourth picture shows No 549 in 1980 at the Steine with a Southdown 1978-vintage Duple-bodied Leyland Leopard and Brighton Corporation No 36, a Weymann Orion-bodied PD3 of 1968.

Finally we see three Brighton & Hove double-deckers circumnavigating the Old Steine in 2010.

Trolleybuses arrived in Brighton in 1939 when 44 handsome Weymann-bodied AECs were delivered. Others arrived after the war, together with three Weymann-bodied BUTs for Brighton, Hove & District, the only ones ever owned by a member of the Tilling Group. No 9 stands at the Steine on 22 May 1956.

Trolleybuses were abandoned in 1961, but some of the post-war BUTs were sold to Maidstone Corporation, which kept operating electric vehicles until 1967. LCD 52 was preserved, in Maidstone colours, and is seen here operating at Carleton Colville Museum, that East Anglian Mecca for tram and trolleybus enthusiasts, in 2001.

Edward Street Garage was the principal Southdown garage in the Brighton area, and is seen here in 1973 with two of the Park Royal-bodied PD2s of 1955, No 769 leading, that had been demoted to training duties, retaining their apple green and primrose livery but bearing the NBC logo. Inside are an assortment of PD3s, VRs and Leopards.

The 'present' view shows the building that now occupies the site of Edward Street Garage.

One of the most spectacular buildings in all of England, and one that has come to symbolise Brighton, is Nash's Royal Pavilion. Originally a farmhouse, it was rebuilt by John Nash in what was referred to as the 'Hindoo' style. Brighton & Hove Leyland National No 152 of 1986, sporting the 'Metro' insignia, heads past shortly before withdrawal in 2000.

Scania Omnilink K230 No 54 *John Peckham* is seen at the same location in April 2011. John Peckham is probably the oldest Brighton resident of whom we have records. Born around 1230 into a poor family, he nevertheless rose to become one of the most distinguished of the 13th-century Archbishops of Canterbury.

Madeira Drive is the name bestowed on the avenue that forms the promenade east of the Steine and the Palace Pier. In this view looking across Madeira Drive towards the Palace Pier in November 1998, an Excelsior coach from Bournemouth is drawn up. Volks Railway, the oldest electric railway in England, has gone into retirement until next spring.

Looking in the opposite direction from the Palace Pier to Madeira Drive in the summer of 2010, four coaches are parked, while above on Martine Parade a Brighton & Hove Scania double-decker is heading towards Rottingdean.

No 102, a Southdown Leyland N-type with solid tyres of 1919 with a later – but not much later – Dodson body, takes a breather in Madeira Drive on 21 October 1922.

The second view is of Madeira Drive 34 years later, on 22 May 1956. Whole-day and half-day excursions traditionally touted for business here, and at the front of the queue is No 1268, a Leyland PS1 Tiger of 1947. This particular style of body was not one of Harrington's finest, having a somewhat overblown appearance. *Pamlin/MHCB*

On 14 November 2010 a gathering of preserved Southdown vehicles took place beside the not very welcoming sea at Brighton. Seen on a distinctly damp Madeira Drive are Harrington-bodied Leyland TS7 Tiger No 1179 of 1937, Park Royal-bodied TD5 No 248 of 1939, VRs Nos 510 of 1971 and 272 of 1981, and PD3 971 of 1964.

In 1997 a family disembarks at Madeira Drive opposite a former London Transport RMC Green Line coach converted to open-top format.

Every first Sunday in May the Historic Commercial Vehicle Club stages a run from London to Brighton and the entrants then go on display along Madeira Drive. Maidstone & District CO558, a Leyland TS7 Tiger of 1937 with a 1950-vintage Harrington body, is seen arriving during an overcast May 2000. The indicator proclaims that it is working the South Coast Express, a service that regularly brought Maidstone & District coaches to Brighton.

Open-top double-deckers have long been part of the Brighton scene. No 5994, a Bristol K5G of 1938, originally with Bristol, was bought by Brighton, Hove & District in 1955 and rebuilt to the form seen here at the far end of Madeira Drive on 22 May 1956.

Open-top single-deckers are rare compared to their double-deck counterparts, but this is Maidstone & District OR 2, a Beadle-bodied AEC Regal of 1946, converted to this format at Hastings in 1957 for work further along the coast. It entered preservation in 1983 and is seen here having taken part in the HCVC run in 2002.

Awaiting their next call of duty in Pool Valley on 22 May 1956 are all-Leyland PD2 Titan No 710 of 1951 and No 183, a Leyland TD5 Titan of 1938 with a 1947 Saunders body. The 8-feet-wide Farington bodies fitted to Titans 701-54 in 1951-53 had wind-down windows at a time when most companies other than London Transport were fitting slide vents, and were adorned in that beautiful Southdown livery, in the author's opinion just about as handsome as a double-deck bus could get.

On Sunday 14 November 2010 apple green and primrose buses and coaches reappeared in Pool Valley after an absence of many decades. No 786, a Beadle-bodied Leyland PD2 Titan of 1956, negotiates the narrow entrance leading from the Steine.

In the third view preserved TS7 coach No 1179 and PD2 Titan No 186 pose in Pool Valley on 14 November 2010.

No 188, a 1938-vintage Leyland TD5 Titan with an original Beadle lowbridge body, stands in Pool Valley in about 1948, a year before a replacement highbridge body was fitted. *Author's collection*

In Pool Valley on 1 June 1960 we see the Southdown double-decker in all its half-cab glory with, from right to left, No 783, a Beadle-bodied PD2 Titan of 1956; 732, an all-Leyland Farington-bodied PD2 of 1951; 239, a TD5 of 1939 with a Park Royal body of 1949; 506, an all Leyland PD2 of 1948; and two 1956 Park Royal Arabs. Three others have nearly made it into the picture.

Finally we see Pool Valley in November 2010, with two National Express coaches. *Author's collection/MHCB(2)*

At the same time as Brighton Corporation replaced its trams by trolleybuses in 1939 it invested in a fleet of 21 Weymann-bodied AEC Regents. No 61 is being overtaken by a stylish Vauxhall Wyvern on Marine Parade on 22 May 1956.

The Weymann-bodied Regent of the immediate pre-war and early post-war days was a true classic, and probably reached its apogee when adorned in the dignified red and cream livery of Brighton Corporation. Some of the 1939 Regents served the town – as it then was – for more than 20 years and we are fortunate that No 63, seen here, has been preserved, originally by Michael Dryhurst, to demonstrate just how these stylish buses complemented the most stylish town on the South Coast.

Perhaps the finest novel set in an English seaside town is Graham Greene's *Brighton Rock*. It presents a very different Brighton from the elegant terraces, grand hotels and electric Pullman trains, instead focussing on the day-tripper from working-class suburbs, good-time girls and, in particular, the violence that was associated with racecourse gangs in the 1930s. Brighton, Hove & District No 6361, an ECW-bodied Bristol K5G of 1940, is ready outside the Conway Street Works to set off for the racecourse.

Being a Tilling company from way back, Brighton, Hove & District was a great patron of Bristol buses. Virtually *the* standard bus of the early post-war years was the K-type fitted with the highbridge version of the standard ECW body. No 6447, dating from 1953, has been preserved by the Brighton & Hove Bus Company. *Author's collection/MHCB*

The annual Historic Commercial Vehicle Club run from London to Brighton on the first Sunday in May is both part of the Brighton Festival – together with Gay Pride marches, open houses, comedians, art shows, you name it, Brighton has it – and one of the highlights of the lorry, fire-engine and bus enthusiast's year. Tilling ST922 of 1930, an open-staircase AEC Regent, now owned by the London Bus Preservation Trust, would have felt very much at home when it reached its destination in 1971, for identical vehicles worked in Brighton from 1930 into the post-war years.

MO 9324, seen in the second picture, is a former Thames Valley Tilling-Stevens B9A of 1927 with a replica body built by

those extraordinary and dedicated chaps at Amberley Museum, and is seen here on one of its first outings after completion, approaching Brighton on a very wet May morning in 1999. It had been withdrawn in 1939, but the outbreak of war gave it a new life, often conveying GWR employees evacuated from Paddington to outlying Berkshire villages to work at Reading. It then passed to a farmer, or rather his chickens, before being rescued and brought to Sussex.

Vastly better weather greets Countryliner Dennis Dart No 130 at the same location on the A23 on the evening of 20 May 2011.

Passing through Preston Park on the 1995 HCVC run is No 928, a Short Bros-bodied Leyland TD1 Titan of 1931. This rather handsome bus, somewhat more curvaceous than contemporary Leyland bodies, was sold by Southdown in 1940, but continued work for another 19 years. I saw it being towed near Bolney in the late 1960s, looking pretty sorry for itself, but in 1987 it found a home at Amberley. It still has all its original running units, having passed straight from passenger service to preservation, although the body has needed substantial tender loving care.

Heading home through Preston Park on its way back to London, having taken part in the 2010 HCVC run, is the only surviving London Transport six-wheel double-decker, LT165, an AEC Renown of 1931. It is part of the London Transport Collection, which it entered straight from passenger service in 1949 and is thus in remarkably original condition.

As is obvious from this picture, Brighton is a very hilly city, and away from the grandeur of the Royal Pavilion, the seafront hotels and terraces, there are rows and rows of what were originally workers' terraced houses; a disorientated stranger might easily think himself in a Lancashire cotton town. No 544, a Park Royal-bodied Guy Arab of 1956, pounds up such a street a few months before withdrawal in 1971.

The 38 route, although altered slightly, still scales the heights today, as this Plaxton Pointer-bodied Dennis Dart demonstrates in April 2011.

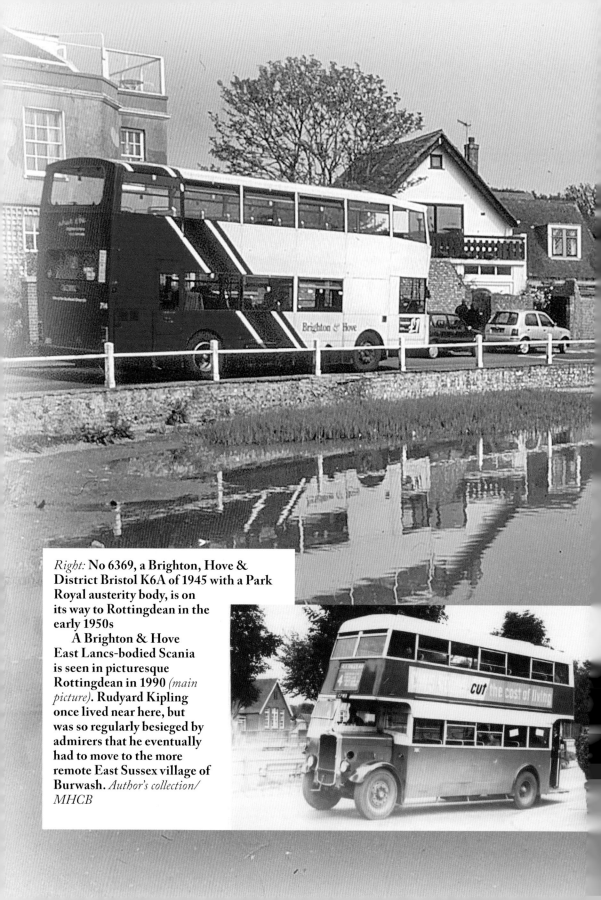

Right: **No 6369, a Brighton, Hove & District Bristol K6A of 1945 with a Park Royal austerity body, is on its way to Rottingdean in the early 1950s**

A Brighton & Hove East Lancs-bodied Scania is seen in picturesque Rottingdean in 1990 *(main picture).* **Rudyard Kipling once lived near here, but was so regularly besieged by admirers that he eventually had to move to the more remote East Sussex village of Burwash.** *Author's collection/ MHCB*

Somewhat surprisingly, Brighton, Hove & District bought six Dennis Lance double-deckers, with Tilling bodies, in 1935. Dennis single-deckers were familiar enough in Sussex and Kent, but the double-deck Lance was a rare beast outside Aldershot & District territory. Brand new No 6311 is seen here at Conway Street, Brighton, looking very grand, all done up in cream livery to celebrate the Silver Jubilee of King George V and Queen Mary. The six Lances lasted 14 years, so they must have been considered a reasonable investment. *Author's collection*

Lewes

Parked outside Lewes bus station in about 1958 is Leyland Titan No 254 of 1939 with a Northern Counties body of 1950; it is working route 25, which took the inland route from Brighton to Eastbourne by way of Lewes, Berwick and Polegate. The bus station, a neat, if unassuming edifice, was completed in 1954.

Right: The bus station is seen again in February 2011. On the right is a Countryliner Dart, while alongside the building is a Lewes Rider Optare Solo working route 121 to Sheffield Park, with a Rider Dart behind. There are some attractive gardens at Sheffield Park, but in 1954 these would not have warranted sufficient traffic to feature as a terminus. It is, of course, the Bluebell Railway heritage line that is the big draw; back in 1954 Sheffield Park was merely a little-used station on a doomed branch line. Sadly, today Lewes bus station is nothing short of a disgrace. Neglected and officially closed – according to a tatty notice stuck in the window – that doesn't seem to have stopped buses loading and unloading there, as you can see, but in a town that takes great pride in its hundreds, if not thousands, of handsome buildings, large and small, its bus station does it no credit whatsoever. *Jack Turley, Dinnages/MHCB*

Above: **Opposite the bus station was the garage, and inside in 1971 is No 1222, a Beadle-bodied Leyland Tiger Cub coach of 1958. It is surrounded by other, more modern coaches, all in store for the winter.**

Disposed of long ago, the garage is now no longer is use as can be seen in this picture, taken through a gap in the door, in February 2011.

In the 21st century a modest resurgence of apple green and primrose reappeared on Renown company buses. The Optare Spectra was always a rather handsome design, and one is seen here to great effect on YJ51 ZVK, a DAF of 2001, climbs the steep High Street in the summer of 2009 working the 143 to Eastbourne; the 143 more or less replaces Southdown route 25, which we saw the TD5 working some 55 years earlier. Renown was founded as a coach company in Bexhill in 1962, but of late has been operating a number of bus services in Sussex and elsewhere.

More commonly seen today climbing High Street are Brighton & Hove Bus Company double-deckers such as No 679 *Dr William King*, a Scania with an East Lancs Omnidekka body, photographed in February 2011. Who was Dr King, you ask? Well, he was not only a physician living in Brighton in the early part of the 19th century, but also a philanthropist and, together with Robert Owen, a founder of the Co-operative movement, another reminder that Brighton was very much a town of working people, many of whom had to struggle to keep their families' bodies and souls together.

No 205, an East Lancs-bodied PD2 Titan of 1955, bowls along the A26 between Uckfield and Lewes on its way from Tunbridge Wells to Brighton in 1969.

Fifty-six years later, in February 2011, Brighton Bus Company No 678 *Jack Howe* is seen between Uckfield and Lewes operating service 29, the successor to the 119. Jack Howe was a welfare officer in Brighton, but is chiefly remembered as a children's entertainer and for doing much for the poor children of the town. He died in 1976.

Haywards Heath

Haywards Heath is an important railway junction. The main lines from London to Brighton and Eastbourne separate to the south, and the secondary route from London by way of East Grinstead and Horsted Keynes used to come in from the north; a section remains open for freight, and one day the Bluebell Railway may once again work passenger traffic over it and restore the passenger connection. Consequently bus services have always called at or terminated there. In the station yard in July 1954 two pre-war Southdown Titans, TD4 No 148 of 1936 with a Northern Counties body of 1950, and TD5 No 221 of 1939 with an East Lancs body, also from 1950; they are working respectively route 82 to Crawley, and 84, a local circular service.

At the station in 1988 is a Mercedes minibus; these featured briefly in the Southdown fleet in the 1980s. No 914, in a livery reminiscent of the old apple green and chrome yellow, even sporting 'Southdown' in an approximation of the script once used, is loading up. The railway station entrance is immediately behind the bus, and the top of the bus station, built in 1956, can just be seen on the extreme left of the picture.

Although there is still a bus stop beside the station, it doesn't seem to get a lot of use and cars occupy where the two Titans were taking their ease in 1954. A Countryliner Dart sneaks past in April 2011.

The Southdown garage in Haywards Heath was located not all that far from the bus station, in Gordon Road, and lasted from 1926 to 1988. Wearing its 16 years lightly, No 1207, a Leyland Tiger of 1938 with a Park Royal 32-seat body, poses outside the garage. Although Harringtons provided the vast majority of coach bodies in the 1930s, Park Royal built several batches on Tigers, Cubs and Cheetahs, that on the Tigers being virtually indistinguishable from the Harrington product. I choose the word 'pose' deliberately, for a young mechanic, noting my interest in his charges, drove a selection of them out of the garage so that I could take their portraits.

Residential accommodation now occupies the site, the garage having been demolished in 1988.

Eventually Southdown, after a long love affair with Leyland PD3s, succumbed to the charms, such as they were, of ECW-bodied Bristol VRs. No 501, seen here in South Road, Haywards Heath, is passing Victoria Park when brand new. It arrived in 1970, together with five others. It was actually preceded by ten VRs the previous year, but these had been ordered by Brighton, Hove & District, not arriving until after the Southdown takeover.

Not quite so new is Countryliner Dart YT51 EAE of 2001, heading along South Road in April 2011. *Author's collection/MHCB*

Beachy Head

No 1242, a Plaxton-bodied Leyland Leopard 49-seat coach of 1968 on a half-day excursion, heads through the South Downs behind the Birling Gap in 1970. On the horizon is Belle Tout, a lighthouse built in 1834, decommissioned in 1902, and used for a variety of purposes in the subsequent years.

In the second view, looking from the top of Beachy Head towards Belle Tout on the morning of 8 August 2011, a Brighton & Hove Scania on route 13X climbs towards Beachy Head. At one time filmed and owned by the BBC, the lighthouse is now a hotel.

The Traffic Commissioners having deemed that the route up to Beachy Head was 'unsuitable for double-deckers', in 1934 Southdown ordered two 40-seat six-wheel TS6T Tigers, and added another two TS7Ts in 1935 to work it. One of the latter, No 53, is seen at Beachy Head in 1950. *Author's collection*

On 8 August 2011 two Brighton & Hove Scanias working service 13X pause at the top of Beachy Head. Also getting into the picture is the inevitable ice-cream van and tourist coach. The view from here, however many times repeated, is simply breathtaking. On this particular beautiful Monday morning it was possible to just make out, far to the east, the nuclear power station at Dungeness in Kent, and, to the west, beyond the tower blocks of Brighton and the great curve of the Sussex coast, Selsey Bill, a span of more than 50 miles. *Author's collection/MHCB*

In 1974 No 294, a 1966-vintage Southdown PD3, begins the steep descent behind Beachy Head, where the South Downs come to a dramatic end, with Eastbourne spread out beyond.

At the same location in May 2009 Brighton & Hove Scania No 906 *James Gray* tackles the ascent. James Gray was a noted collector and taker of photographs who, in his long life – he died in 1998 at the age of 96 – amassed a collection of 9,000 pictures of Brighton and Hove, which are now being put on line.

Eastbourne

Eastbourne Corporation operated the first municipal motor bus service in the world in April 1903. Less cosmopolitan than Brighton, it is nevertheless a town with character and some fine buildings along the seafront, a splendid new art gallery, and a spectacular setting against the Downs to the west, in contrast to the east, which stretches to the edge of the Pevensey Marshes, reaching several inches above sea level here and there. No 94, an all-Leyland TD4c Titan of 1936 converted to open-top in 1952, is heading for the foot of Beachy Head in about 1955; that was as near as Corporation

buses were allowed, Southdown being granted the licence to run to the top of Beachy Head. No 94 was withdrawn in 1961 after a career of 25 years. At this time Eastbourne took great care of its buses and kept many in service for 20 or more years. *Author's collection*

This is the same location on 7 August 2011, but looking in the opposite direction. This was a day when vintage Eastbourne buses were out and about. In the foreground is former Corporation Leyland Lion No 12, dating from 1939. One of four identical buses,

fitted with Leyland bodywork, three were requisitioned by the War Office and never returned, but No 12 had a long life with the Corporation. Never overworked, I used to see it pottering about the town in the 1960s and, when eventually withdrawn after serving Eastbourne for 28 years, it immediately passed into preservation. In the distance, turning below Beachy Head where No 94 was in our previous picture, is preserved Corporation AEC Regent III No 42, with rare Bruce bodywork of 1951, while a City Sightseeing open-topper is on the left.

Crossleys were uncommon, although not unknown, in southern England. Eastbourne Corporation bought eight DD42/5s with East Lancs bodies in 1948. However, they don't seem to have been as well thought of as Regents or Titans, and all had been withdrawn by the end of the 1963 summer season. Route 4 was a circular service.

Also heading for Archery, spinning along the Royal Parade east of the pier in 1967, is an East Lancs-bodied PD1 of 1946/47 converted to open-top format in 1961/63, one of the successors to the TD4 open-toppers. *Author's collection/MHCB*

In the third view, from 7 August 2011 *(right),* another open-topper, preserved RT3435 of 1952 of the London Bus Company, is seen passing the Glastonbury Hotel on the Royal Parade, where your author met his wife in the summer of 1967.

Finally *(above),* at the same location on the same day is No 69, an Eastbourne Corporation AEC Regent Mark V with East Lancs bodywork of 1963.

Opposite Eastbourne's elegant pier in 1969, waiting for holidaymakers to climb aboard to either explore the delights of the town or make the dizzying climb to the top of Beachy Head, are Corporation No 60, an East Lancs-bodied AEC Regent V of 1961, and Southdown No 406, a convertible Northern Counties-bodied PD3 of 1964.

Some five years later, standing side-by-side at the same location, are Corporation No 80, an East Lancs-bodied PD2A/30 of 1966, and Southdown No 2051, a former Brighton, Hove & District convertible Bristol/ECW Lodekka of 1963.

Beside the pier in the third photograph, with Bexhill-on-Sea in the far distance beyond Pevensey Bay, is No 1234, a Southdown Plaxton Panorama-bodied Leyland Leopard coach in National Express white in 1976.

At the same location 33 years later we see *Dame Anita Roddick*, of Body Shop fame, alias Brighton Bus Company Scania Omnidekka No 912.

This is Pevensey Road Bus Station, Eastbourne, in 1969. Two Southdown Marshall-bodied Leopards are ready to depart, No 682 of 1968 for East Grinstead and No 164 of 1967 for Brighton. A few years earlier both routes would have been worked by double-deckers.

In 2009 Eastbourne Buses DAF M441 CCD passes the spot where the bus station once stood.

Eastbourne Corporation No 24, an AEC Mark III Regent with a Weymann body of 1947, heads past the railway station on its way to Old Town in 1956. This handsome bus served the citizens of Eastbourne for 20 years. *Author's collection*

Fifty-three years later, in 2009, we see two Corporation buses in variations of blue in front of the railway station. On the left is No 35, a Plaxton Pointer-bodied Dennis Dart, and on the right No 70, a MAN with MCV Evolution bodywork. *Author's collection/MHCB*

Hailsham

Top: Hailsham is an ancient market town, a working town with a mixture of distinctive buildings dating back the best part of a thousand years, but with many of Victorian and 20th-century origin. The main London to Eastbourne road used to pass through, as did the railway line from London to Eastbourne by way of Oxted and Heathfield. The latter disappeared, despite much protest, in the 1960s, while some ten years earlier a bypass took through road traffic away. No 1784, a Southdown Duple-bodied Leyland Leopard of 1967, pauses outside the modest 1960s shopping mall while working an afternoon tour in 1969.

Opposite: At the same location in 1975 is No 232, a short-wheelbase Bristol RE with a Marshall 43-seat body of 1968. The 92 was one of a number of long-established Southdown routes from the Sussex Coast to towns in the north of the county, where they connected either with Maidstone & District, London Transport Country Buses or Aldershot & District. Most have vanished; today an hourly service connects Eastbourne and Uckfield, where a change is necessary to the rather infrequent Countryliner to East Grinstead.

Above: On 12 May 2011 practically all that seems to have changed is the vehicles – the passengers hardly at all! With the takeover of Eastbourne Corporation, which worked into Hailsham for many years, Stagecoach, Southdown's successor, reappeared. An Alexander/Dennis Enviro 300 takes a breather before returning to Eastbourne.

No 3753, a Maidstone & District AEC Reliance with a Weymann BET-style body of 1965, makes haste along the Hailsham bypass in 1969 on its way to Tunbridge Wells on a joint Maidstone & District/Southdown service. The dignified dark green and pale cream livery suited this design to a T.

The replacement of the direct Eastbourne to Tunbridge Wells service in 2011 is Stagecoach 51, which terminates at Heathfield, with a connection there for Tunbridge Wells. On 12 May 2011 a Stagecoach Dennis Trident/Alexander ALX400 speeds along the tree-lined bypass; in a hundred yards or so it will swing right into Hailsham town centre.

Hailsham Garage was built as late as 1957. Fourteen years later it was gone, the shortest-lived, surely, of all Southdown establishments. Harrington-bodied Leopard No 1745 and a PD3 are at ease inside in 1970 – many shades of green.

Closed in 1971 Hailsham Garage was replaced by these residential buildings, with a reminder of past times is its title, Southdown Court.

Uckfield

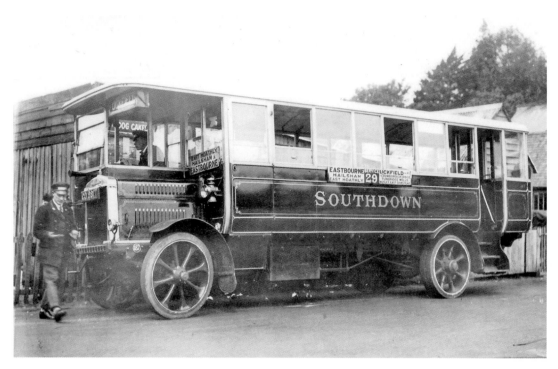

Southdown No 187, a 1925-vintage Leyland SG11 with Tilling bodywork, stands at Uckfield on 23 August 1926. It is working the 29, which in those days connected East Grinstead with Eastbourne.

One evening in 1971, Southdown No 808, an East Lancs-bodied Leyland PD2 Titan of 1957, pauses at Uckfield bus station on its way to Brighton.

Today the bus station has moved a short way to the west, behind the main road. Brighton Bus Company No 683 *Terence Morgan* turns in towards it in February 2011. Terence Morgan was a British actor who often played the villain in films of the 1940s and 1950s and later ran a hotel in Brighton. *Pamlin/MHCB (2)*

The 119 was jointly operated by Southdown and Maidstone & District. In 1977 ECW-bodied Bristol VR No 5113 of the latter company climbs the steep hill out of Uckfield on its way from Tunbridge Wells to Brighton on the 729 service, successor to the 119. The bus station can be seen at the bottom of the hill playing host to a number of Southdown Leopards.

Renown's FN54 FLC, a Transbus Dart with a Caetano body in the local authority-supported Rider livery, is at the same location in 2011. Not a great deal has changed in Uckfield, although there is now a bypass, and today the signal box at the bottom of the hill is a taxi office, and the level crossing, which caused so many hold-ups on summer weekends, has being removed when the section of railway between Uckfield and Lewes was closed in 1968. The 318 connects Uckfield with Heathfield, Burwash and Hurst Green.

Between Uckfield and Crowborough the 119 climbed up to Ashdown Forest, an area not of densely packed trees but a mixture of clearings and coppices – once, although it is difficult to believe, the heart of industrial England and the iron industry. If you know where to look, the remains of the medieval ironworks can still be found. So worried was Elizabeth I about the rate that trees were being cut down to feed the furnaces, and thus denude the shipyards of oak to build warships to keep the Spanish at bay, that she imposed strict quotas. No 805, a Southdown East Lancs-bodied PD2 of 1957, heads across the forest in 1970.

The road network out of Uckfield has changed greatly in the intervening 45 years. The Brighton & Hove Scania Omnidekka that we met earlier in Uckfield heads across the forest on the 29, the successor to the 119, on a grey February afternoon in 2011. A. A. Milne, who lived on the northern edge of Ashdown Forest, and Ernest Shepard, his illustrator, who lived some 15 miles away on the North Downs, immortalised the area by setting the stories of Winnie-the-Pooh and Christopher Robin's other animals there. On any day there are bound to be children visiting the Forest simply to play 'Poohsticks' on one of the streams that bisect it.

Forest Row

At the opposite end of the forest is Forest Row. East Surrey ST 1047 stands at the Forest Row terminus of the 409 in 1932. Built a year earlier, these short-wheelbase AEC Regents monopolised the 409 from 1932 until STLs began to take over during the Second World War. *Author's collection*

On 17 April 2011 preserved RT604, recreating RT days on the 409, turns off the A264 past the appropriately named Foresters Arms and heads towards its terminus on the site of Forest Row station, which, despite being Dr Beeching's own, he didn't hesitate to close – there's devotion to unthinking political dogma. RT604 is a particularly historic vehicle. Nominally dating from 1948, it was one of three RTs repainted in National Bus Company livery in 1977 and sent back to Chelsham, the next garage to Godstone whence the 409 mostly worked, for service 403 and 453 duties. It lasted until 1978, and it is generally accepted that by this date it was the oldest bus in regular service in the entire National Bus Company fleet. It passed directly into preservation, lives locally, and is a regular on the rally circuit. *Author's collection/ MHCB*

East Grinstead

Recreating the old Southdown route 87 is the preserved Maidstone & District Harrington-bodied AEC Reliance of 1958, standing at the site of the old East Grinstead bus station, now a car park, on 17 April 2011, ready to work to Forest Row. Harringtons fitted a bus-type front to this coach in 1963, going out of their way, it would appear, to make the match as incongruous as possible, as can be seen. The handsome livery is a compensation, and one is delighted that the old monster is still with us after much remedial work by the dedicated preservationists.

East Grinstead was the one town in Sussex where London Transport, Southdown and Maidstone & District bus services all met regularly. London Transport and Southdown both had garages in the town, and Maidstone & District buses laid over in the Southdown one. At the bus station in 1976 is, on the left, Southdown Leopard No 195 of 1968, and on the right London Country Leyland National SNC 85 of 1973, downgraded from Green Line duties, and not a day too soon.

Today the former principal service out of East Grinstead by Maidstone & District, the 91 to Tunbridge Wells, is now the 291, seen here worked by Metrobus's rather stylish Scania Omnicity No 627 of 2008 passing through Forest Row in March 2011. It is about to leave the A22 London to

Eastbourne Road and swing east onto the A264, which runs along the edge of Ashdown Forest, past the house where A. A. Milne, his wife, Christopher Robin, Winnie-the-Pooh, Tigger et al lived, through Hartfield, Withyham and Groombridge, and over the border into Kent.

Seen again parked outside East Grinstead Garage in 1974 is brand new (as if that signifies) Leyland National coach SNC 85, about to set off on the long and not very comfortable journey to Hemel Hempstead, while behind stands RF75, a one-time and rather more suitable Green Line coach of 1951, relegated to bus work.

London Country's East Grinstead Garage was demolished in 1981 and replaced by this block of flats, seen in March 2011.

For the best part of 90 years Croydon has been connected to East Grinstead by the 409. Seen at Purley in 1950 on its way south is London Transport Country Area front-entrance STL1446B (the 'B' indicating that it was in use as a bus rather than on Green line duties, despite that being fairly obvious), dating from 1936. *Author's collection*

Metrobus Dart/Caetano No 377 of 2001 picks up passengers at Caterham station on its way to East Grinstead on 24 March 2011. From here on it will follow the time-honoured 409 route through Godstone to East Grinstead, but the northern section is now quite different. Passenger take-up has dropped steadily over the years – it is much quicker to Purley and Croydon by train – and by the time this volume is published the 409 may have been cut right back to run just between Dormansland and East Grinstead.

Most 409 journeys continued on from East Grinstead to Forest Row. Despite being close to Kent, East Grinstead is actually in West Sussex, and it was only on the long sweep down the A22 on the approach to Forest Row that the 409 crossed into East Sussex, as seen here through the window of an RT. RTs worked the 409 from 1949 until replaced by Routemasters in 1965, and occasionally after that. *Author's collection/MHCB*

Reluctantly London Transport decided that it had to dip its toe into one-person operation, and in 1965 bought 50 rear-engined Leyland Atlanteans and six Daimler Fleetlines. The more successful Fleetlines gravitated to East Grinstead Garage, where they mainly operated the 424, although they occasionally appeared on the 409. XF7 is seen here in 1975 in East Grinstead High Street.

Thirty-six years later preserved XF3 recreates the scene, although not everything is the same, as the National Westminster Bank has become a restaurant (although there is still a branch elsewhere in the town). It has to be said that Park Royal went to great lengths to produce one of the ugliest bus bodies ever seen and scored a perfect bullseye.

The icing – or rather complete lack of – on the cake was that the interior appointments were also way below usual London Transport standards. That is to take nothing away from the preservationists, for ugly or not the XF had a key role to play in the development of the London bus and it is right and proper that at least one example should survive.

Crawley

In 1931 Southdown built refreshment rooms at Royal Oak, just north of Crawley on the A23 and approximately halfway between London and Brighton, at the not inconsiderable cost of £10,000. The London to Brighton run was by far the company's busiest long-distance route, and the refreshment rooms did a roaring trade. No 1017 (left), a Leyland TS2 Tiger of 1931 with a later Harrington body, and No 1235, an ECW-bodied Leyland PS1 Tiger of 1947, are seen awaiting their refreshed passengers in about 1950. *Author's collection*

The cost of Southdown's refreshment rooms may have caused the company's accountant a few extra grey hairs, but £10,000 would probably have hardly covered the cost of executive soap in Astral Towers, which now stands on the site. Gatwick Airport is a few hundred metres to the north. *Author's collection/MHCB*

This is the London Country garage at Northgate Rd, off the A23 at Crawley, in November 1973. Just visible on the left is the front end of Maidstone & District Harrington-bodied AEC Reliance coach No 4437 of 1960, while centre stage is shabby-looking RT4767 of 1954, with an Atlantean and an RML in the distance.

The very last active member of London Transport's T Class of AEC Regals, in production from 1929 to 1948, worked out of Crawley Garage until August 1962. Preserved T792 is the sole survivor of this final version, dating from 1948.

Crawley was a very small garage and most of its occupants had to be parked in the yard outside. In London Country days in the late 1970s, at a time when the company was struggling to provide a reliable service, the third picture, of a diverse assembly of vehicles of varying ages and conditions, illustrates the problems it was facing. From left to right are Atlantean AN7, bearing a very 'non-PC' all-

over advert livery, in front of a dead RF and an equally lifeless Merlin, then former Green Line double-deck coach RCL2249 and Swift SMW1, a bus acquired from South Wales in 1971.

The garage closed in the early 1980s, and the area has seen much redevelopment. Scania Omnicity No 573 heads towards the town centre along the A23 close to the site of the garage on 20 May 2011.

Bexhill

Cooden Beach, Bexhill, was the western extremity of the Hastings Tramways network. No 32, a 1947-vintage Weymann-bodied Sunbeam trolleybus, enters the loop at the terminus in about 1955. The trams had been replaced by trolleybuses in the late 1920s, and Maidstone & District took over the company in 1935. It was operated as an independent concern almost until the end, in 1957, when a fleet of Atlanteans brought to an end electric road passenger transport (milk floats excepted) in Bexhill, St Leonards and Hastings.

Public transport no longer quite reaches this location. A rather more upmarket form of transport – well, some would consider it so – is seen in the second picture *(above left)* approaching the previous location on 12 May 2011.

Today route 96 almost reaches Cooden Beach station but, according to a notice posted at the bus stop, parking of private cars in the loop outside has of late prevented buses turning there, so on 12 May 2011 an elderly Optare Solo of Renown, but nicely done up in something very close to traditional Southdown livery, is about to turn right and head away from Cooden beach. *Author's collection/MHCB (2)*

Maidstone & District DH161, a wartime Bristol K6A, updated in 1953 with this attractive Weymann body, is seen in Sidley, in the suburbs of Bexhill, on 25 June 1957.

In what might almost be a time warp, apart of course from the bus, this is the same location on 12 May 2011. Fifty-four years on, Candy Corner, albeit with a new fascia, is still there, and the railings have been renewed. Otherwise time seems to have passed by this corner of Sussex. The bus is a Volvo B10M with a Plaxton Paladin body reliveried to bring attention to St Michael's Hospice.

St Leonards

This is Bulverhythe Depot, Bexhill Road, St Leonards-on-Sea, in October 1954. Used by trolleybuses until 1940, then by the Army, from 1947 onwards Maidstone & District used it to store buses due for scrapping. In this sad line-up are a Leyland Titan TD4 and four Titan TD5s. The former is No 225 with a Short Bros body dating from 1935, the latter are Nos 260, 255, 266 and 263, Weymann-bodied TD5s of 1939.

The second view shows the site of the former Bulverhythe depot in January 2011.

Hastings Tramways Park Royal-bodied Sunbeam trolleybus No 23 of 1946 heads along St Leonards Marina on a wintry day in January 1948 calculated to keep the most ardent visitor indoors.

In rather less inclement weather 63 years later, in January 2011, Stagecoach R654HCD is seen at the same location. *Author's collection/MHCB*

Hastings

In Hastings town centre in about 1954, Park Royal-bodied Sunbeam trolleybus No 21 of 1946, bound for Silverhill Depot, leads Saunders-bodied Bristol K6A No DH219 of 1948 on local service 27. Both route numbers are contained within a circle, a feature that persisted well into the 1950s.

In 2008, a little further along to the east, we see the unique *Happy Harold of Hastings*. This 1928-vintage Guy trolleybus with an open-top Dodson body entered the service fleet in 1940, then re-entered passenger service in 1953 and became quite a celebrity, a status it still enjoys. With the end of trolleybuses in Hastings it was preserved, and in 1960 was fitted with a Commer TS3 diesel engine. Since then it was appeared regularly at carnivals, special events and rallies. *Author's collection/MHCB*

Ex-London Transport Leyland Titans were quite a feature of the Stagecoach fleet on the Sussex coast in the 1990s. Here No 7287 heads along Carlisle Parade, Hastings, in 1999.

In the second photograph a Stagecoach Dart turns out of Albert Road into Carlisle Parade in February 2011. The poor old pier looks extremely sad after a disastrous fire on 5 October 2010, which destroyed 95% of it, ironically one day after plans for its redevelopment had been invited. It had been closed for safety reasons since 2006.

Stagecoach Titan No 7290 loads up in Carlisle Road in Hastings town centre in 1999.

Marks & Spencer, for reasons best known to itself – probably on the instructions of the indestructible Twiggy! – now calls itself 'M&S', which makes no difference to Rider Solo YJ05 WCF in February 2011.

A view looking down the funicular at Hastings East Cliff in 1951. Built in 1903, it was at this time operated by water power, the water being stored in two towers at the top. Below are seven coaches, among which are a Southdown Leyland Tiger, two AEC Regals, what must be a brand-new Burlingham Seagull, a normal-control Austin and a Leyland Comet.

In the same view in February 2011 the area has been somewhat altered, but the unique fishermen's storage sheds remain a feature; coaches no longer park there. The funicular was converted to electric power in the 1970s, extensively refurbished in 2008, new cars being provided, and was reopened in 2010. It is the steepest funicular in the United Kingdom. *Author's collection/MHCB*

DH271, a Weymann-bodied Bristol K6A of 1949, stands at Hastings railway station, terminus of local route 27, in October 1954.

Fifty-seven later Hastings railway station has been much modernised and the road layout changed drastically; a Stagecoach Solo, loading up on local service 20A, stands outside the station on a January evening in 2011.

Rye

Rye was one of the Cinque Ports and many would consider it the county's most picturesque town. There was a time when East Kent's territory extended across the Sussex border into Hastings, and the company's only garage in the county was in Rye. Here three of the company's Park Royal-bodied Dennis Lancet 3s of 1947, CFN 124/139/140 (East Kent did not use fleet numbers at this time) turn their backs to the camera at the rear of the garage in about 1955.

The second photograph is of preserved East Kent Weymann-bodied AEC Reliance KFN 220 of 1955.

Finally we see a view of the former East Kent garage at Undercliff, Rye, in early 2011. Opened in October 1932, it was transferred to Maidstone & District in 1975. Since 1981 it has been owned by Alsford Timber, and until the 1980s timber was imported direct into Rye from Scandinavia. It still comes by ship but not to Rye, which is no longer a commercial port.
Author's collection/MHCB (2)

East Kent JG 9924, a Leyland TD5 of 1938, rebodied in 1949 by Park Royal, is seen at Rye on its way to Camber in about 1954. On the right is a Weymann-bodied AEC Reliance of 1955, identical to the one in the picture on the previous page.

In the summer of 1999, heading for Camber Sands and almost across the border into Kent, is Stagecoach Alexander-bodied Olympian N388 LPN of 1995.

At the same location, but looking south-eastwards along Romney Marsh towards Kent in January 2011, is a Stagecoach Enviro 400 working route 100 'The Wave' towards Hythe, Folkestone and Dover. *Author's collection/MHCB*

At Rye station in 2000 Stagecoach Alexander-bodied Olympian No 358 of 1995 is working the 711 service from Dover to Brighton. On the left is a Plaxton-bodied coach of Empress, a Hastings firm founded in 1929.

At the same location in January 2011, N60 HAM, a Volvo of Hams coaches, is working a railway replacement service. Hams, a family firm founded in 1962, is based at Flimwell in East Sussex.